P9-APY-980

Deportes y actividades/Sports and Activities

¡Vamos a jugar al básquetbol!

Let's Play Basketball!

por/by Carol K. Lindeen

Editora consultora/Consulting Editor: Gail Saunders-Smith, PhD

Consultora/Consultant: Kymm Ballard, MA
Consultora de Educación Física, Atletismo y Medicina Deportiva
Departamento de Instrucción Pública de Carolina del Norte/
Physical Education, Athletics, and Sports Medicine Consultant
North Carolina Department of Public Instruction

CAPSTONE PRESS
a capstone imprint

Pebble Plus is published by Capstone Press,
1710 Roe Crest Drive, North Mankato, Minnesota 56003.
www.capstonepub.com

Copyright © 2012 by Capstone Press, a Capstone imprint. All rights reserved.
No part of this publication may be reproduced in whole or in part, or stored in a retrieval system, or
transmitted in any form or by any means, electronic, mechanical, photocopying, recording, or otherwise,
without written permission of the publisher. For information regarding permission, write to Capstone Press,
1710 Roe Crest Drive, North Mankato, Minnesota 56003.

 Books published by Capstone Press are manufactured with paper
containing at least 10 percent post-consumer waste.

Library of Congress Cataloging-in-Publication Data
Lindeen, Carol, 1976–
  ¡Vamos a jugar al basquetbol! = Let's play basketball! / by Carol K. Lindeen.
     p. cm.
  Includes index.
  Summary: "Simple text and photographs present the skills, equipment, and safety concerns of basketball—in
both English and Spanish"—Provided by publisher.
  ISBN 978-1-4296-8246-6 (library binding)
  1. Basketball—Juvenile literature. I. Title. II. Title: Let's play basketball!
GV885.1.L4943 2012
796.323—dc23   2011028798

Editorial Credits
Heather Adamson, editor; Strictly Spanish, translation services; Kia Adams, designer; Eric Manske, bilingual
    book designer; Kelly Garvin, photo researcher; Kathy McColley, production specialist

Photo Credits
All photos Capstone Press/Karon Dubke except page 13, Shutterstock/Klementiev Alexey

Note to Parents and Teachers

The Deportes y actividades/Sports and Activities set supports national physical
education standards related to recognizing movement forms and exhibiting a physically
active lifestyle. This book describes and illustrates basketball in both English and
Spanish. The images support early readers in understanding the text. The repetition of
words and phrases helps early readers learn new words. This book also introduces early
readers to subject-specific vocabulary words, which are defined in the Glossary section.
Early readers may need assistance to read some words and to use the Table of Contents,
Glossary, Internet Sites, and Index sections of the book.

Printed in the United States of America
102011   006405CGS12

Table of Contents

Tabla de contenidos

Playing Basketball

Pass, shoot, swish!

Basketball players

play as a team.

Juguemos al básquetbol

¡Pasa, lanza, tiro limpio!

Los jugadores de básquetbol

juegan en equipo.

Basketball players dribble
the ball as they run.
They throw and catch.
They pass the ball.

Los jugadores de básquetbol
driblan la pelota mientras corren.
Ellos lanzan y atrapan.
Ellos pasan la pelota.

Basketball players jump.
They try to get by the
other players. They shoot
the ball into the hoop.

Los jugadores de básquetbol saltan.
Tratan de esquivar a otros jugadores.
Ellos lanzan la pelota al aro.

Players score points
for making baskets.
Baskets count for one,
two, or three points.

Los jugadores anotan
puntos al hacer canastas.
Las canastas cuentan por
uno, dos o tres puntos.

Equipment

Basketballs are easy to bounce and catch. They are made of rubber and covered with bumpy grips.

Equipo

Las pelotas de básquetbol son fáciles de rebotar y atrapar. Están hechas de goma y cubiertas por granulaciones de agarre.

Basketball hoops have
a backboard and a net.
Hoops are at the ends
of flat courts.

Los aros de básquetbol tienen
un tablero y una red. Los aros
de básquetbol están en los
extremos de canchas planas.

Safety

Basketball players guard each other carefully. They try not to push or shove.

Seguridad

Los jugadores de básquetbol se marcan unos a los otros cuidadosamente. Ellos no tratan de empujar o agarrarse entre sí.

Basketball players rest.
They drink water and wait
for their turn to play.

Los jugadores de básquetbol
descansan. Ellos beben agua y
esperan su turno para jugar.

Having Fun

Dribble, pass,

jump, and shoot.

Let's play basketball!

Vamos a divertirnos

Dribla, pasa, salta

y lanza. ¡Vamos a

jugar al básquetbol!

Glossary

basket—a score made in basketball when a player throws the basketball through the hoop; baskets can be worth 1, 2, or 3 points

court—a flat space for playing a ball game; a basketball court is shaped like a rectangle with one basket at each end

dribble—to bounce the ball with one hand while moving down the court

guard—to use your arms and body to try to keep a player on the other team from getting the ball or shooting; basketball players cannot push, grab, or trip players they guard

hoop—a round ring on a backboard; a basketball hoop is a metal circle with a net hanging from it

pass—to bounce or throw the ball to another person on the same team

shoot—to throw or toss the basketball toward the hoop

Internet Sites

FactHound offers a safe, fun way to find Internet sites related to this book. All of the sites on FactHound have been researched by our staff.

Here's all you do:

Visit *www.facthound.com*

Type in this code: 9781429682466

Check out projects, games and lots more at
www.capstonekids.com

Glosario

el aro—un anillo redondo en un tablero; un aro de básquetbol es un círculo metálico con una red colgando de este

la canasta—un punto anotado en básquetbol cuando un jugador lanza la pelota a través del aro; las canastas pueden valer 1, 2, o 3 puntos

la cancha—un espacio plano para jugar un partido de pelota; una cancha de básquetbol tiene la forma de un rectángulo con una canasta en cada extremo

driblar—rebotar la pelota con una mano mientras se corre en la cancha

lanzar—tirar o enviar la pelota de básquetbol hacia el aro

marcar—usar los brazos y el cuerpo para tratar de evitar que un jugador del otro equipo reciba la pelota o haga un lanzamiento; los jugadores de básquetbol no pueden empujar, agarrar o hacer tropezar a jugadores mientras marcan

pasar—rebotar o lanzar la pelota hacia otra persona del mismo equipo

Sitios de Internet

FactHound brinda una forma segura y divertida de encontrar sitios de Internet relacionados con este libro. Todos los sitios en FactHound han sido investigados por nuestro personal.

Esto es todo lo que tienes que hacer:

Visita *www.facthound.com*

Ingresa este código: 9781429682466

¡Algo súper divertido! Hay proyectos, juegos y mucho más en www.capstonekids.com

Index

Índice